MW01173836

voices of faith
for a new millennium

voices of faith
for a new millennium

365 DAILY REMINDERS

COMPILED BY

Judith Couchman

VINE
BOOKS

SERVANT PUBLICATIONS
ANN ARBOR, MICHIGAN

Vine Books is an imprint of Servant Publications especially designed to serve evangelical Christians.

Reminder number 64 is taken from *The Place of Help* by Oswald Chambers, © 1989 by the Oswald Chambers Publications Assoc. Ltd, and is used by permission of Discovery House Publishers, Box 3566, Grand Rapids, MI 49501. All rights reserved.

Published by Servant Publications
P.O. Box 8617
Ann Arbor, Michigan 48107

Compiled by Judith Couchman.

99 00 01 02 10 9 8 7 6 5 4 3 2 1

ISBN 1-56955-162-6
Printed in the United States of America

Cataloging-in-Publication Data on file at the Library of Congress.

1

God made me in His image
so that I dare to speak up
about my uniqueness.

MIRIAM ADENEY

2

The call of God upon us is
to share His mission in the
world.

JOSEPH C. ALDRICH

3

The study of God's Word,
for the purpose of discover-
ing God's will, is the secret
discipline which has formed
the greatest characters.

JAMES W. ALEXANDER

4

And in His will is our peace.

DANTE ALIGHIERI

5

When you say a situation or a person is hopeless,
you are slamming the door in the face of God.

CHARLES L. ALLEN

6

The heavens—with all of their incessant witness to God's
glory—never tell of the loyal love of God. The trees and
flowers—with all of their messages of God's wisdom—
describe nothing of God's saving action in Jesus Christ,
His last Word. It is in the Scriptures, *and in them alone,*
that we meet God as a Person.

RONALD B. ALLEN

7

Although God's holiness and His law are relentlessly
demanding and we cannot, at any moment, live righteously
enough in our own holiness to please Him,
He provides a way of escape through offering His Son
as a covering for our sin.

DAN ALLENDER

8

The Holy Spirit is born from Love and is of Love, all its
treasures are of Love, and if we are to believe our Gospels it
is received by Love and Love only.

FLORENCE ALLSHORN

9

You may trust the Lord too little
but you can never trust Him too much.

ANONYMOUS

10

God may well be taken as a substitute for everything;
but nothing can be taken as a substitute for God.

ANONYMOUS

11

The only important decision we have to make
is to live with God; He will make the rest.

ANONYMOUS

12

God is great, and therefore He will be sought;
He is good, and therefore He will be found.

ANONYMOUS

13

In all His dispensations God is at work for our good. In prosperity He tries our gratitude; in mediocrity, our contentment; in misfortune, our submission; in darkness, our faith; under temptation, our steadfastness; and at all times, our obedience and trust in Him.

ANONYMOUS

14

When you come to face the thing you fear, trust the Creator.

ANONYMOUS

15

God does not ask about our ability or our inability, but our availability.

THE ARKANSAS BAPTIST

16

If we wait upon the Lord, He will give us strength beyond
human understanding.

BILL ARMSTRONG

17

God loves you greatly and is waiting to bless your life with
all of His eternal goodness. He is waiting for you to take the
first step toward Him and all He has to offer you.

STEVE ARTERBURN

18

Are you weak? Weary? Confused? Troubled? Pressured?
How is your relationship with God? Is it held in its place of
priority? I believe the greater the pressure, the greater your
need for time alone with Him.

KAY ARTHUR

19

Thou hast made us for Thyself, and the heart of man
is restless until it finds its rest in Thee.

AUGUSTINE

20

Speak thou to Him for He heareth,
And spirit with spirit will meet!
Nearer is He than breathing,
Nearer than hands and feet.

MALTBIE D. BABCOCK

21

Every believer is God's miracle.

PHILIP JAMES BAILEY

22

The fact of Jesus' coming is the final and unanswerable proof
that God cares.

WILLIAM BARCLAY

23

Our eternal salvation may be secured by the initial decision
to accept Christ's forgiveness, but conversion is the lifelong
process of turning away from our plans and turning toward
God's maddening, disruptive creativity.

M. CRAIG BARNES

24

Jesus does not give recipes that show the way to God as
other teachers of religion do. He is himself the way.

KARL BARTH

25

God asks so little of us and promises so much. We need only
look to God with a mustard seed of faith, and God works
through us mightily.

DAVID BECKMANN

26

The very word "God" suggests care, kindness, goodness;
and the idea of God in His infinity is infinite care, infinite
kindness, infinite goodness. We give God the name of good;
it is only by shortening it that it becomes God.

HENRY WARD BEECHER

27

It is one thing to be the advocate of Christianity, and another
to be the disciple of it. And though it may sound strange at
first, far easier is it to teach its lessons than to learn them.

J.G. BELLETT

28

We are always seeking the reason. We want to know why.
But God does not reveal His plan—He reveals Himself.

BOB BENSON

29

God does not force Himself on any of us. He has given us
free wills and capacity for decision making. We are invited to
open ourselves so He can enter our lives. Our thought lives,
our conversations, our actions, and our relationships become
opportunities for God to glorify Himself.

KARIN BERENBERG

30

Our sense of sin is in proportion to our nearness to God.

THOMAS D. BERNARD

31

God develops character to match
His assignments. If you can't be
faithful in a little, God will not
give you a larger assignment.

**HENRY T. BLACKABY
AND CLAUDE V. KING**

32

God appears and God is light
To those poor souls who dwell in night;
But does a human form display
To those who dwell in realms of day.

WILLIAM BLAKE

33

Take thy first walk with God!
Let Him go forth with thee;
By stream, or sea, or mountain path,
Seek still His company.

HORATIUS BONAR

34

If you dismiss the word of God's command,
you will not receive His word of grace.
How can you hope to enter into communion with Him
when at some point in your life you are running away
from Him? The man who disobeys cannot believe,
for only He who obeys can believe.

DIETRICH BONHOEFFER

35

Adoration is the lifting up of the heart and mind to God,
asking nothing but to enjoy God's presence.

THE BOOK OF COMMON PRAYER

36

If you will work *for* God, form a committee.
If you will work *with* God, form a prayer group.

CORRIE TEN BOOM

37

To be little *with* God is to be little *for* God. It takes much
time for the fullness of God to flow into the spirit.
Short devotions cut the pipe of God's full flow.
We live shabbily because we pray meagerly.

E.M. BOUNDS

38

The difference between duty and love is that the first
represents Sinai and the second represents Calvary.

RICHARD BRAUNSTEIN

39

We are brought into God's Kingdom by grace; we are sanctified by grace; we receive both temporal and spiritual blessings by grace; we are motivated to obedience by grace; we are called to serve and, finally, we are glorified by grace. The entire Christian life is lived under the reign of God's grace.

JERRY BRIDGES

40

All God wants of His followers is that we love Him with all our heart, soul, mind, and strength and that we trust His promises and obey His commands. He will then give us wisdom, grace, favor, manpower, finances—everything we need—to accomplish all that He has called us to do.

BILL BRIGHT

41

I believe God, through His Spirit, grants us love, joy, and peace no matter what is happening in our lives. As Christians, we shouldn't expect our joy to always feel like happiness, but instead recognize joy as an inner security— a safeness in our life with Christ.

JILL BRISCOE

42

The Christian who rejoices in the all-sufficient power of the Spirit of God within draws the biggest temptation and the greatest opposition. That is why some Christians don't want to be dangerous, and they turn down the opportunity for God's kind of adventure. They prefer to be comfortable.

STUART BRISCOE

43

Do not pray for easier lives;
Pray to become stronger men.
Do not pray for tasks equal to your powers;
Pray for powers equal to your tasks.

Then your life shall be no miracle,
But you shall be a miracle.
Every day you shall wonder
At that which is wrought in you
By the grace of God.

PHILLIPS BROOKS

44

Earth's crammed with heaven,
And every common bush afire with God.
And only he who sees takes off his shoes,
The rest sit round and pluck blackberries.

ELIZABETH BARRETT BROWNING

45

If I stoop
Into a dark tremendous sea of cloud,
It is but for a time; I press God's
    lamp
Close to my breast; its splendor,
    soon or late,
Will pierce the gloom: I shall emerge
    one day.

ROBERT BROWNING

46

Spiritual power begins with the surrender of the
individual to God. It commences with obedience
to the first commandment.

WILLIAM JENNINGS BRYAN

47

The believer can handle the world's temptations and walk
before God in victory over the world. It is certain that we
must remain a part of the world system until our Lord calls
us home to heaven. Our victory over the world is ours to
claim while we live it here and now.

MARK I. BUBECK

48

Our loving God has created each one of us to do
best that which we enjoy doing.

JAMIE BUCKINGHAM

49

It is He who made us and not we ourselves, made us out of
His peace to live in peace, out of His light to dwell in light,
out of His love to be above all things loved and loving.

FREDERICK BUECHNER

50

Spiritual gifts are desirable, but great grace and small gifts are
better than great gifts and no grace.

JOHN BUNYAN

51

When we surrender every area of our lives—including
our finances—to God, then we are free to trust Him to
meet our needs. But if we would rather hold tightly to
those things that we possess, then we find ourselves
in bondage to those very things.

LARRY BURKETT

52

Trust God for great things; with your five loaves and two
fishes, He will show you a way to feed thousands.

HORACE BUSHNELL

53

We cannot get away from God,
though we can ignore Him.

WILLIAM ALLEN BUTLER

54

Contrition is not easy work: it is surgery. But, like surgery, it is not an end in itself: the wise prayer of confession always leads to an acceptance of God's pardon.

GEORGE A. BUTTRICK

55

If thou knowest God, thou knowest that everything is possible for God to do.

CALLIMACHUS

56

Faith is the knowledge of the benevolence of God toward us, and a certain persuasion of His veracity.

JOHN CALVIN

57

God never said that He would lay out His plan for your life in cinemascope so you can view it in its entirety. What He does promise is to lead you as you go; to direct you day by day; to show you His will hour by hour.

TONY CAMPOLO

58

Beyond the preoccupation we all have with our needs, the rock-bottom reality of prayer is the sharing of experience. No experience—neither that of joy nor of sorrow—is full and complete until it is shared with God.

MICHAEL CARD

59

The very act of praise releases the power of God into
a set of circumstances and enables God to
change them if this is his design.

MERLIN CAROTHERS

60

Being born again is new life, not of perfection but of
striving, stretching, and searching—a life of intimacy
with God through the Holy Spirit. There must first be
an emptying, and then a refilling. To the extent that
we want to know, understand, and experience God,
we can find all this in Jesus.

JIMMY CARTER

61

There are but two classes of the wise; the men who serve
God because they have found Him, and the men who seek
Him because they have found Him not.

RICHARD CECIL

62

Among the many attributes of God, although they are all
equal, mercy shines with even more brilliance than justice.

MIGUEL DE CERVANTES

63

We are just as spiritual when resting, playing, sleeping, ill, or
incapacitated, if it is His will for us, as when we are directly
serving God. We can maintain an undercurrent of knowing
that we are in complete accord with God and pleasing to
Him whatever we are doing.

LEWIS SPERRY CHAFER

64

If I maintain communion with God
and recognize that He is taking me up
into His purposes, I will no longer try
to find out what those purposes are.
If God has been brave enough to
trust me, surely it is up to me not
to let Him down, but to "hang in."

OSWALD CHAMBERS

65

God is not a symbol of goodness.
Goodness is a symbol of God.

G.K. CHESTERTON

66

God gave His only begotten Son to be crucified on the
cross so that this world could be saved and redeemed.
That is God's uppermost goal—the redemption of souls.
So when you desire divine healing, or an answer from above,
always focus through the lenses of the uppermost goal,
the redeeming of souls.

DAVID YONGGI CHO

67

It's exciting to live in complete oneness with the will of God.
It is never dull or static because it is not a one-time,
once-for-all commitment. It is something we have
to work at constantly, moment by moment.

EVELYN CHRISTENSON

68

The most important thing in any prayer is not what we say
to God, but what God says to us. We are apt to pray and
then hurry away without giving God a chance to answer.

CHRISTIAN ADVOCATE

69

God has no grandchildren;
either you know Him firsthand
or you do not know Him at all.

CHRISTIAN LIFE

70

God is not so well pleased with being our Master as
He is with being our Father; He is not so pleased
with our being His slaves as He is with being His children.
This is what God truly wants.

JOHN CHRYSOSTOM

71

When our hearts are tenderly responsive …
and it suits His greater plan, then the Lord will lift
the thin veil that separates us. And we will be
stunned to realize that He has been closer
than our own breath all along.

PATSY CLAIRMONT

72

'Twas God the Word that spake it;
He took the Bread and brake it;
And what the Word did make it;
That I believe, and take it.

S. CLARKE

73

God loves us *in* our sin,
and *through* our sin,
and goes on loving us,
looking for a response.

DONALD COGGAN

74

Holiness is the only possible response to God's grace.
Holy living is loving God.

CHARLES COLSON

75

Living a life of love is the wise choice of a person
who has accepted God-given power.

BARBARA COOK

76

If we're willing to listen to what the Creator says rather
than what we want to hear, if we're committed to
knowing Him and His plans for us instead of demanding
our own way, He will speak. God confides in the
person with a "hearing heart."

JUDITH COUCHMAN

77

I have committed myself and my all into God's hands,
and He has accepted the offering.
Life henceforth can never be the same.

CHARLES E. COWMAN

78

God provides resting places as well as working places.
Rest, then, and be thankful when He brings you,
wearied, to a wayside well.

MRS. CHARLES E. COWMAN

79

God moves in a mysterious way
His wonders to perform;
He plants His footsteps in the sea
And rides upon the storm.

WILLIAM COWPER

80

Confession gives us a time and place to remember a single moment when we know that we brought our sins to Jesus to be covered by His blood. Remembering our confession helps us to have a clean slate with God.

NEVA COYLE

81

The more clearly we recognize how we dig our own wells in search of water, the more fully we can repent of our self-sufficiency and turn to God in obedient trust.

LARRY CRABB

82

O perfect redemption, the purchase of blood—
To every believer, the promise of God.

FANNY J. CROSBY

83

The truth of the gospel is intended to free us
to love God and others with our whole heart.

BRENT CURTIS AND JOHN ELDREDGE

84

What a comfort to know that our lot is cast by the Lord, our
gifts are of His appointing, and our life work planned way
back there in eternity! Such assurance does not
lead to inaction; it leads to freedom of action
with the right kind of confidence.

ARTHUR CUSTANCE

85

I do not believe that there is such a thing in the
history of God's kingdom as a right prayer offered
in a right spirit that is forever left unanswered.

THEODORE L. CUYLER

86

If we wait upon God, there is no danger. If we rush on, He
must let us see the consequences of it.

JOHN DARBY

87

To be a Christian is to be reborn, and free,
and unafraid, and immortally young.

JOY DAVIDMAN

88

God makes all chosen souls pass through a fearful
time of poverty, misery, and nothingness.
He desires to destroy in them gradually all the help
and confidence they derive from themselves so that He
may be their sole source of support, their confidence,
their hope, their only resource.

JEAN-PIERRE DE CAUSSADE

89

The most miserable person on the face of the earth is the
Christian who is trying to enjoy both worlds.

EDWARD DENNETT

90

Each day is new, yesterday is gone,
and God is the God of a second chance.
Though others may fail and disappoint,
He never will.

RUTH GRAHAM DIENERT

91

To accept his kingdom and to enter in brings blessedness,
because the best conceivable thing is that we should
be in obedience to the will of God.

CHARLES HAROLD DODD

92

One of the most convenient hieroglyphics of God is a circle;
and a circle is endless; whom God loves, He loves to the
end; and not for their own end, to their death, but to His
end; and His end is that He might love them all.

JOHN DONNE

93

God's love for poor sinners is very wonderful, but God's
patience with ill-natured saints is a deeper mystery.

HENRY DRUMMOND

94

Let us sit at the feet of God. Let us listen for His Word. Let
us turn to the lives of some of the heroes of faith to see how
they were able to see God's power released and God's
answers made known.

WESLEY L. DUEWEL

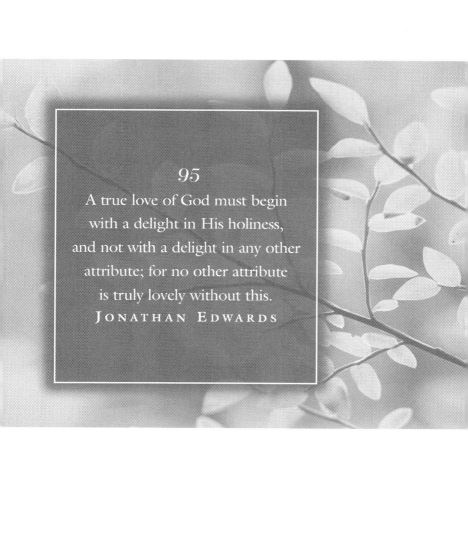

95

A true love of God must begin
with a delight in His holiness,
and not with a delight in any other
attribute; for no other attribute
is truly lovely without this.

JONATHAN EDWARDS

voices of faith for a new millennium

96
He is no fool who gives what he cannot keep
to gain what he cannot lose.
JIM ELLIOT

97
All I have seen teaches me to trust the Creator
for all I have not seen.
RALPH WALDO EMERSON

98
Obedience to God is the most infallible evidence of sincere
and supreme love to Him.
NATHANAEL EMMONS

99

God is without limits. Nothing is impossible with Him. He is the author of true creativity. All creation is His, including every idea our minds can conceive. He keenly desires to give us the ability to make the right choices in our lives.

TED ENGSTROM

100

When you have shut the doors and made a darkness within, remember never to say that you are alone; for you are not alone, but God is within.

EPICTETUS

101

Faith is not a sense, nor sight, nor reason,
but taking God at His Word.

ARTHUR EVANS

102

Humility opens the way to God and joy. Pride stands back,
hands at its sides, and says, "No, thanks, I can do it myself."
Humility comes with hands outstretched.

COLLEEN TOWNSEND EVANS

103

Following the Lord's commands is more than dutiful doing.
Through actively walking with God, we are conformed to
His will; and as we walk, our faith to follow Him increases.
By freely responding to the grace of obedience with our
whole hearts, we enter a realm of trust in God.

DEBRA EVANS

104

There is hardly ever a complete silence in the soul.
God is whispering to us well-nigh incessantly.
Whenever the sounds of the world die out in the soul,
or sink low, then we hear the whisperings of God.

F.W. FABER

105

God encourages us in the long, slow process of transformation to full spiritual sonship. He has predestined
us to be conformed to the image of His Son! Christ
has prayed that we may share in His glory!

SINCLAIR B. FERGUSON

106

A state of mind that sees God in everything is evidence
of growth in grace and a thankful heart.

CHARLES FINNEY

107

God does not respond to persistence because we have managed to wrest His blessing from Him, or have convinced Him that we are unworthily worthy, or have annoyed Him to the point that He succumbs to our demands. God responds to persistence because it communicates earnestness and singular desire.

JEAN FLEMING

108

We must not be content to be cleansed from sin; we must be filled with the Spirit.

JOHN FLETCHER

109

The Christian is made to be responsive to the nature of God. All who come near him should sense the presence and love of God.

WILLIAM FLETCHER

110

His love has no limit;
   His grace has no measure;
His pow'r has no boundary known
   unto men.
For out of His infinite riches in Jesus,
He giveth, and giveth, and giveth again!

ANNIE JOHNSON FLINT

111

The Word of God is in the Bible
   as the soul is in the body.

PETER TAYLOR FORSYTH

112

Prayer is the soul getting into contact
with the God in whom it believes.

HARRY EMERSON FOSDICK

113

God receives us just as we are and accepts our prayers just as they are. In the same way that a small child cannot draw a bad picture, so a child of God cannot offer a bad prayer.

RICHARD J. FOSTER

114

Let the one that buys, or sells, or possesses, or uses this world be as if he did not. Let them be master over the world in the power of the Spirit of God, and let them know that they owe no one anything but love.

GEORGE FOX

115

The Creator loves you very much since He gives you so many good things. Therefore, be careful not to be ungrateful, but strive always to praise God.

FRANCIS OF ASSISI

116
....

We can trust God to fulfill the Bible's promises
in His way and on His timetable.

CHERI FULLER

117
....

God gave and so should we. And our loving and
our giving should have no limiting boundaries,
just as God's love has none.

MILLARD FULLER

118
....

Men conceive they can manage their sins with secrecy;
but they carry about them a letter, or book rather,
written by God's finger, their conscience
bearing witness to all their actions.

THOMAS FULLER

119

It pleases the Father that all fullness should be in Christ;
therefore there is nothing but emptiness anywhere else.

W. GADSBY

120

Love is God's essence; power but His attribute; therefore is
His love greater than His power.

RICHARD GARNETT

121

We believe that Christ is God not because He mysteriously
possessed a divine nature united to a human, but because as
man we find God in Him, and God finds us through Him.

A.E. GARVIE

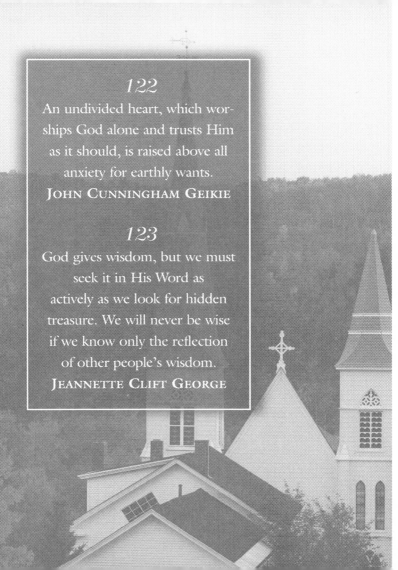

122

An undivided heart, which worships God alone and trusts Him as it should, is raised above all anxiety for earthly wants.

JOHN CUNNINGHAM GEIKIE

123

God gives wisdom, but we must seek it in His Word as actively as we look for hidden treasure. We will never be wise if we know only the reflection of other people's wisdom.

JEANNETTE CLIFT GEORGE

124

God says whatever the length of our lives, we will be satisfied
with what He gives us, for real life never ends.

PETER E. GILLQUIST

125

Like Palestine, the landscape of God's kingdom is sloped so
that its rivers flow to the lowest valleys.

The valleys are people whose lives are eroding away.

The river is mercy.

KEN GIRE

126

God calls us to be His disciples, laborers, soldiers, ambassa-
dors, witnesses, workers, servants, and disciplemakers....
But, joyfully, He [also] calls us to be His beloved bride.

JUDY GOMOLL

127

It's safe to trust God's methods and to go by His clock.

S.D. GORDON

128

In the midst of trials we can thank God because we know
He has promised to be with us, and He will help us.
We know that He can use times of suffering to draw us
closer to Himself. I don't know what trials you may be
facing right now, but God does. He loves you.

BILLY GRAHAM

129

Death, that final curb on freedom, has itself suffered
a death blow through the resurrection of Jesus.

MICHAEL GREEN

130

What the Lord is asking me, He is asking no one else….
Yet even as He asks it, He makes it clear that He will give
me the power to do what is needed.

EMILIE GRIFFIN

131

A Christian is somebody who trusts in the holiness and
righteousness of God and, particularly, in what God has
done in Christ, reconciling the world to Himself by Jesus'
death on the cross. A Christian's trust is not in his own character or actions but in the character and actions of God.

MICHAEL GRIFFITHS

132

Every action performed in the sight of God because it is the
will of God, and in the manner that God wills, is a prayer.

JEAN-NICHOLAS GROU

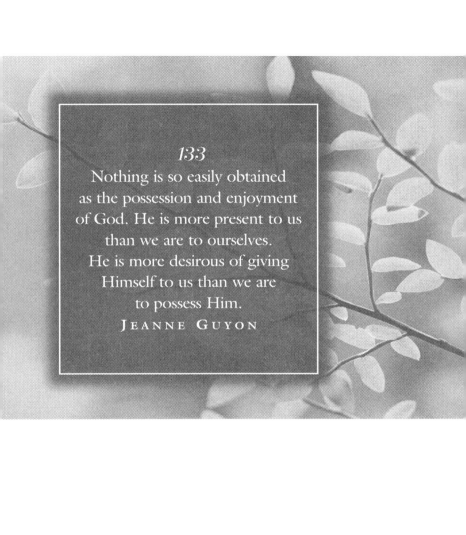

133
Nothing is so easily obtained
as the possession and enjoyment
of God. He is more present to us
than we are to ourselves.
He is more desirous of giving
Himself to us than we are
to possess Him.

JEANNE GUYON

134

As long as we are conscious of our helplessness we will not be overtaken by any difficulty, disturbed by any distress, or frightened by any hindrance. We will … give God the opportunity to help us in our helplessness by means of the miraculous powers which are at His disposal.

OLE HALLESBY

135

Godliness is seeing things as God does: the things of this world as good in that they add comfort to our short stay on this earth, but as secondary in importance to the real things which are spiritual and eternal. Godliness is using the good things of this life as God would, as a means for bringing the blessing to others.

MAXINE HANCOCK

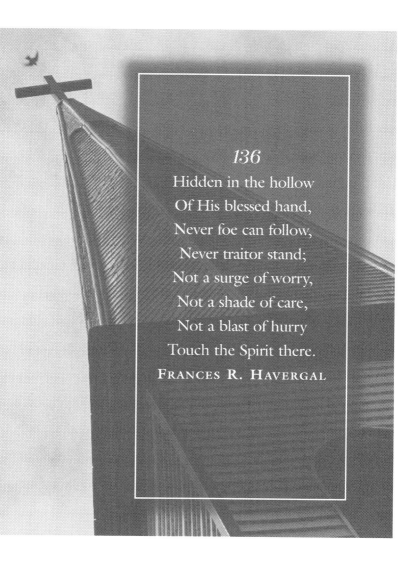

136

Hidden in the hollow
Of His blessed hand,
Never foe can follow,
Never traitor stand;
Not a surge of worry,
Not a shade of care,
Not a blast of hurry
Touch the Spirit there.

FRANCES R. HAVERGAL

137

Perhaps this is the essence of intimacy: not being satisfied or
complacent, but always desiring to go deeper
into the fullness of God.

CYNTHIA HEALD

138

We will not find God in our homes unless we pray there.

MARGARET HEBBELTHWAITE

139

God is Father; God is King. We are subjects; we are sons.
We occupy both His lap and the space at His feet.

DAVID W. HENDERSON

140

We must depend upon the performance of the promise when all the ways leading up to it are shut up. "For all the promises of God in Him are Yea (yes), and in Him Amen (so be it), unto the glory of God by us."

MATTHEW HENRY

141

God provides for him that trusteth.

GEORGE HERBERT

142

God hath two wings, which he doth ever move,
The one is Mercy, and the next is Love:
Under the first the Sinners ever trust;
And with the last he still directs the Just.

ROBERT HERRICK

143

Our hearts need to be broken, and only when they are
shall we be willing for the confessions, the apologies,
the reconciliations, and the restitutions that are
involved in a true repentance of sin.

ROY HESSION

144

God's love is committed, enduring, and tough! His love is not
weak and wavering, but strong and persistent. And it is His full
intent that our love become durable like His.

JAMES HILT

145

If God be for us, who can be against us? Yea, verily! Mountains
do move and are cast into the sea at our bidding. The apostles
exercised this power and we may exercise it.

F.J. HUEGEL

146
The word which God has written
on every brow is hope.
VICTOR HUGO

147
God's will never takes me where
His grace will not sustain me.
RUTH HUMLECKER

148
Of all people on earth, committed
Christians ought to be the most creative,
for they are indwelt by the Creator.
GLADYS HUNT

149

The promises of God are the powerhouse of blessing, the
eternal tools of God whereby victories are won and character
is carved out of the bedrock of human experience.

And remember, every promise is available.

JOHN HUNTER

150

The gospel was not good advice, but good news.

WILLIAM R. INGE

151

Through the night of doubt and sorrow
Onward goes the pilgrim band,
Singing songs of expectation
Marching to the Promised Land.

BERNHARD INGEMANN

152

From all eternity he has pointed out the true way of life:

Jesus, the Christ.

Jesus Christ, the son of Mary.

INSCRIPTION IN AN EGYPTIAN TOMB

153

God never shuts one door but He opens another.

IRISH PROVERB

154

When you believed the gospel, you were sealed by the Spirit.

God the Father put His stamp upon you, so to speak.

He did this by giving you the Spirit to dwell in you—

He who dwells in us is the seal.

H.A. IRONSIDE

155

He who leaves God out of his reasoning
does not know how to count.

ITALIAN PROVERB

156

Maturity learns to fight battles in the prayer closet.
When we pray, God does the impossible in situations
in ways we never could dream of.

CINDY JACOBS

157

O Lord, renew our spirits and draw our hearts unto yourself,
that our work may not be a burden but a delight.

BENJAMIN JENKS

158

God makes sense of the light and shadow. He imparts His
passion. He spreads His glory through our ordinary lives.
God culls out the excess and offers us simplicity.

MARY JENSEN

159

The sound of laughter is God's hand upon a troubled world.

BARBARA JOHNSON

160

God diligently trails after us without hurrying us. He speaks
to us, letting us know that apart from Him we will never be
complete. Once we commit ourselves to Him, He keeps
after us to obey. He does not just say, "I love you."
He constantly shows us how much.

JAN JOHNSON

161

Tears are agents of resurrection and transformation.
They are a gift and their fruit is always joy.

ALAN JONES

162

Grace is free, but when once you take it you are bound forever
to the Giver, and bound to catch the Spirit of the Giver.

E. STANLEY JONES

163

Help us, Lord, to turn toward You, and in our turning,
find that You have been turned toward us all along.

TIMOTHY JONES

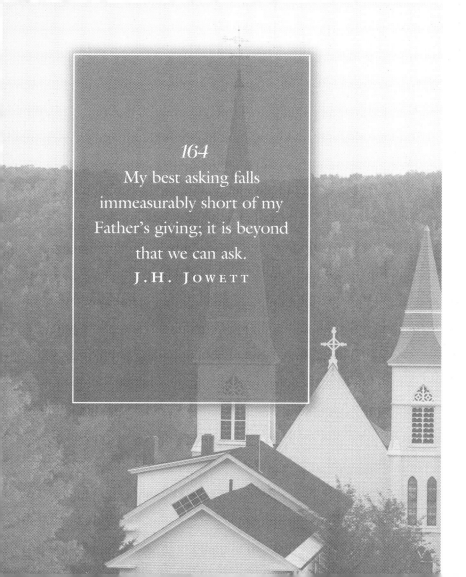

164
My best asking falls
immeasurably short of my
Father's giving; it is beyond
that we can ask.
J . H . J O W E T T

165

Problems are bound to come. But God will be adequate for
any and every situation. Jesus' victory over the spirit of the
world strips fear of its sting. He will give peace.

GIEN KARSSEN

166

Prayer is exhaling the spirit of man and
inhaling the Spirit of God.

EDWIN KEITH

167

It takes some of us a lifetime to learn that Christ,
our Good Shepherd, knows exactly what He is doing with us.
He understands us perfectly.

PHILLIP KELLER

168

God Himself works in our souls, in their deepest depths,
taking increasing control as we are progressively
willing to be prepared for His wonder.

THOMAS KELLY

169

Be thankful for the smallest blessing, and you will deserve to
receive greater. Value the least gifts no less than the greatest,
and simple graces as especial favors. If you remember the
dignity of the Giver, no gift will seem small or mean, for
nothing can be valueless that is given by the most high God.

THOMAS À KEMPIS

170

Teach me to live, that I may dread
The grave as little as my bed;
Teach me to die, the so I may
Rise glorious at that awful day.

THOMAS KEN

171

Ultimately, we don't heal, transform, or create ourselves. We posture ourselves in ways that allow God to heal, transform, and create us. Our part is to learn to sit, yielding to God's activity in us, opening ourselves to divine prayer, listening to the silent words.

SUE MONK KIDD

172

I dare not approach God without a mediator; if my prayer is to be heard, then it will be in the name of Jesus; what gives it strength is that name.

SØREN KIERKEGAARD

173

God is there to meet you in the center of all your trials, and to whisper His secrets, which will make you come forth with a shining face and an indomitable faith that all the demons of hell shall never afterwards cause to waver.

E.A. KILBOURNE

174

Gratitude is from the same root word as "grace,"
which signifies the free and boundless mercy of God.

WILLIS P. KING

175

Take comfort, and recollect however little you and I may know,
God knows; He knows Himself and you and me and all things;
and His mercy is over all His works.

CHARLES KINGSLEY

176

A man with God is always in the majority.

JOHN KNOX

177

Not only will God answer a call but, in His response,
He will go far beyond all that we ask or think.
Our times are in His hands.

C. EVERETT KOOP

178

There is no other reason why our prayers should be
according to the will of God unless our lives may
also be of the same nature.

WILLIAM LAW

179

The world appears very little to a soul that
contemplates the greatness of God. My business is
to remain in the presence of God.

BROTHER LAWRENCE

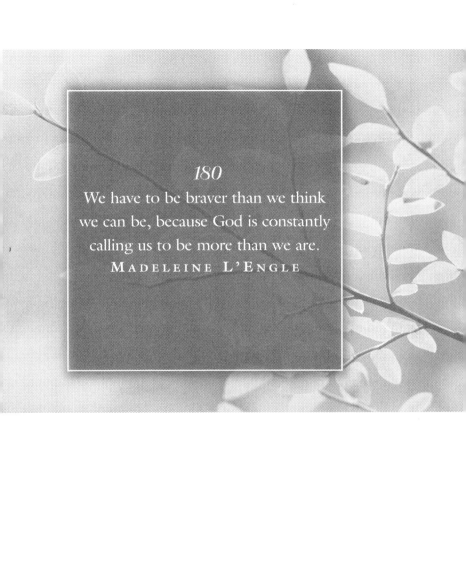

180
We have to be braver than we think
we can be, because God is constantly
calling us to be more than we are.

MADELEINE L'ENGLE

voices of faith for a new millennium

181

Our circumstances are not an accurate reflection of God's goodness. Whether life is good or bad, God's goodness, rooted in His character, is the same.

HELEN GRACE LESCHEID

182

God whispers to us in our pleasures, speaks in our conscience, and shouts in our pain. It is His megaphone to rouse a deaf world.

C.S. LEWIS

183

Nothing is really lost by a life of sacrifice; everything is lost by failure to obey God's call.

HENRY PARRY LIDDON

184

My concern is not whether God is on our side;
my great concern is to be on God's side,
for God is always right.

ABRAHAM LINCOLN

185

Faith recognizes the fact that God is in control of my life.
Whether I believe it or not, it's a fact that God is in
control of the world. If I don't believe it, I'm just
robbing myself of the enjoyment of the fact.

PAUL LITTLE

186

I do not know how the loving Father will bring
out light at last, but He knows, and He will do it.

DAVID LIVINGSTONE

187

Seek happiness and you will never find it. Seek righteousness
and you will find you are happy.

MARTYN LLOYD-JONES

188

Often, in the midst of great problems,
we stop short of the real blessing God has for us,
which is a fresh vision of who He is.

ANNE GRAHAM LOTZ

189

Behind the dim unknown,
Standeth God within the shadow,
keeping watch above His own.

JAMES RUSSELL LOWELL

190

It's our job to hate the sin. But it's God's job to deal with the sinner. God has called us to despise evil, but He's never called us to despise the evildoer.

MAX LUCADO

191

The essence of true holiness consists in conformity to the nature and will of God.

SAMUEL LUCAS

192

When God contemplates some great work, He begins it
by the hand of some poor, weak, human creature to whom
He afterwards gives aid, so that the enemies
who seek to obstruct it are overcome.

MARTIN LUTHER

193

What if we should err on one point or another? What if we dis-
obey God and sin greatly? God will not be caught off guard.
He will not be forced to activate emergency equipment. He is
prepared to help us in our sin as He was to help Adam in his!

ERWIN W. LUTZER

194

How often we look upon God as our last and feeblest
resource! We go to Him because we have nowhere else
to go. And then we learn that the storms of life have
driven us, not upon the rocks, but into the desired haven.

GEORGE MACDONALD

195

God has given us prayer that we might draw close to Him, that
we might share our lives with Him, and that we might see the
miracle of answered prayer each day of our lives.

HOPE MACDONALD

196

The world cannot always understand one's profession of faith,
but it can understand service.

IAN MACLAREN

197

This is the purpose of pain for the redeemed: It is one of your
Father's ways of speaking to you; it is the evidence of His limit-
less love, by which He would draw you farther from evil and
closer to Him, the divine remedy which can cure you of pride
and help you lean more trustingly on the Lord.

WALTER A. MAIER

198

How do we grab aholt of God?
How do we overcome our sadness and isolation?
The answer comes irresistibly and unmistakably: prayer.

BRENNAN MANNING

199

Joy is the echo of God's life within us.

JOSEPH MARMION

200

Unlike earthly kings, God does not want our obedience
out of fear. Our obedience to Him is the fruit of our
lives growing in the rich soil of love and trust. Our
obedience is to be at once both the result of
our loving God and also the proof of our love.

CATHERINE MARSHALL

201

We forget that God sometimes has to say, "No."
We pray to Him as our heavenly Father, and like
wise human fathers, He often says, "No," not
from whim or caprice, but from wisdom and
from love, and knowing what is best for us.

PETER MARSHALL

202

The blessings which the Word of God
leads us to are matchless treasures.
What a joyful trumpet sound it
must be that leads us to them!

COTTON MATHER

203

God has enlarged thee by
the binding of sorrow's chain.

GEORGE MATHESON

204

Without yielding ourselves to Him, we have not, in a
profound sense of the word, received Him as Lord,
even though we know Him as Savior.

JAMES MCCONKEY

205

You can begin to walk out—from wherever you are now—
in the will of God. What joy there is in walking in His will!

J. VERNON MCGEE

206

The feeling of meaninglessness is transformed through
the electrifying declaration that God—the same
God who created the universe—loves us.

ALISTER MCGRATH

207

Obedience to biblical precepts is still the most effective way
to prevent many of the afflictions of mankind.

S.I. McMILLEN

208

Look to the horizon. Do you see the slightest change?
The slightest speck? If you do, follow it,
and God will reveal the rest.

HENRIETTA MEARS

209

While I think of God as a pretty efficient guy,
He doesn't always operate in the fast lane.
He operates quite slowly, in fact, when He needs to.

MARILYN MEBERG

210

Faith is nothing else than trust in the
divine mercy promised in Christ.

PHILIP MELANCTHON

211

There is nothing, indeed, which God will not do for a man
who dares to step out upon what seems to be the mist;
though as he puts his foot down he finds a rock beneath him.

F.B. MEYER

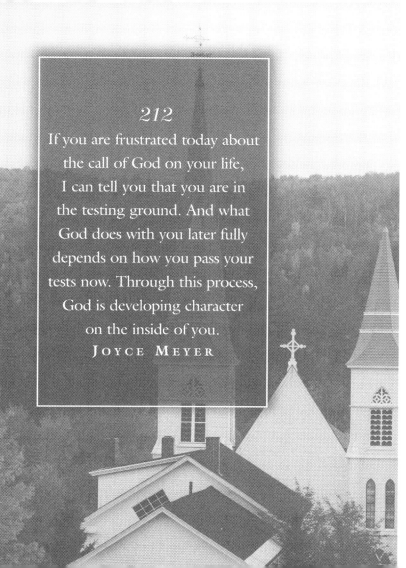

212

If you are frustrated today about the call of God on your life, I can tell you that you are in the testing ground. And what God does with you later fully depends on how you pass your tests now. Through this process, God is developing character on the inside of you.

JOYCE MEYER

213

The mind is a narrow channel, capable of focusing on
only one thought at a time. Therefore if the mind is
focusing on the Word of God, it cannot focus on any
negative or bothersome issue. This in itself is a sound
principle of mental and spiritual health.

CALVIN MILLER

214

It requires a grander heroism to stand and wait and not
lose heart and not lose hope, to submit to the will of God,
to give up work and honors to others, to be quiet, confident,
and rejoicing, while the happy, busy multitude go on and away.

J.R. MILLER

215

Sooner or later putting something or someone in the
center of one's life, where only God belongs, leads a sensitive
person to the end of his or her hope. Evidently, nothing
will give us the safety of the power of God in
our lives, except God.

KEITH MILLER

216

God is the one who clasps your hand as you move
from one place to another. He is the one who has gone
ahead of you, prepared a place for you, and will hold
out His hand for you to cling to.

SUSAN MILLER

217

When we speak of knowing God, it must be understood
with reference to man's limited powers of comprehension.
God, as He really is, is far beyond man's imagination,
let alone understanding. God has revealed only so
much of Himself as our minds can conceive
and the weakness of our nature can bear.

JOHN MILTON

218

Some people think God does not like to be troubled
with our constant asking. The way to trouble
God is not to come at all.

DWIGHT L. MOODY

219

If faith produces no works, I see
That faith is not a living tree.
Thus faith and works together grow;
No separate life they e'er can know:
They're soul and body, hand and heart:
What God hath joined, let no man part.

HANNAH MORE

220

We must live in the atmosphere of the Spirit, high in the
mountains of vision, and there the appetite for the bread
of heaven will be strong, and, feeding upon Christ,
we will "grow up into Him in all things."

G. CAMPBELL MORGAN

221

We cannot possibly be satisfied with anything less—each day, each hour, each moment, in Christ, through the power of the Holy Spirit—than to walk with God.

H.C.G. MOULE

222

"I will wait and see what good God will do to me by it, assured He will do it." Thus we shall bear an honorable testimony before the world, and thus we shall strengthen the hands of others.

GEORGE MÜLLER

223

It is with the heart we must wait upon God. As man's heart is, so is he before God. The message is, "Let your heart take courage, all ye that wait upon the Lord."

ANDREW MURRAY

224

Because you are a special treasure
to God, He is working to draw you
into a deeper love for Him—
away from any idols in your life,
away from rival interests,
away from giving first place to His
good gifts instead of to Him.

RUTH MYERS

225

Some people conceive of Christianity as being all
treasure and no vessel. If sometimes the earthen
vessel is evident in a servant of God, they feel he
is a hopeless case, whereas God's conception is that,
in that very vessel, His treasure should be found.

WATCHMAN NEE

226

There is power in Jesus, but there is no violence.
There is authority, but it is the authority of one
who has taken upon himself the form of a servant.

STEPHEN NEILL

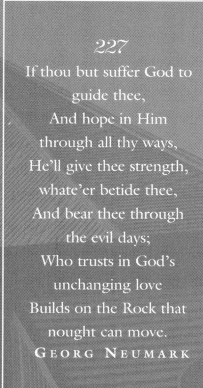

227

If thou but suffer God to
guide thee,
And hope in Him
through all thy ways,
He'll give thee strength,
whate'er betide thee,
And bear thee through
the evil days;
Who trusts in God's
unchanging love
Builds on the Rock that
nought can move.

GEORG NEUMARK

228

When we won't let ourselves be held in the midst of our messes by God who loves us and made us, we miss the unspeakable joy of knowing that we are truly His beloved.

DEBORAH NEWMAN

229

Weak is the effort of my heart
And cold my warmest thought;
But when I see Thee as Thou art,
I'll praise Thee as I ought.

JOHN NEWTON

230

Prayer is not only "the practice of the presence of God,"
it is the realization of His presence.

JOSEPH FORT NEWTON

231

God, give us grace to accept with serenity the things
that cannot be changed, courage to change the
things that should be changed, and the wisdom
to distinguish the one from the other.

REINHOLD NIEBUHR

232

Even in terrible circumstances and calamities, in matters
of life and death, if I sense that I am in the shadow of
God, I find light, so much light that my vision improves
dramatically. I know that holiness is near.

KATHLEEN NORRIS

233

Self-love separates man from God, it blocks the
channels of self-spending and self-offering,
both toward God and toward man.

ANDERS NYGREN

234

One would expect God to applaud our small efforts at
faithfulness; instead a Spirit comes and takes us
where we are not yet prepared to go.

ELIZABETH O'CONNOR

235

Sometimes the Lord rides out the storm with us and other
times He calms the restless sea around us. Most of all, He
calms the storm inside us in our deepest inner soul.

LLOYD JOHN OGILVIE

236

God sees with utter clarity who we are. He is undeceived
as to our warts and wickedness. But when God looks at us
that is not all He sees. He also sees who we are intended
to be, who we will one day become.

JOHN ORTBERG

237

The love of God who is spirit is no
fitful, fluctuating thing, as the love
of man is, nor is it a mere impotent
longing for things that may never be;
it is, rather, a spontaneous
determination of an attitude
freely chosen and firmly fixed.

J.I. PACKER

238

There is no panic in the divine
personality. God is peace,
God gives peace, God gives rest.

JOSEPH PARKER

239

The God of Christians is a God who makes the soul
perceive that He is her only good, that her only rest
is in Him, her only joy in loving Him; who makes her
at the same time abhor the obstacles which withhold
her from loving Him with all her strength.

BLAISE PASCAL

240

No Christian should ever think or say that he
is not fit to be God's instrument, for that in fact
is what it means to be a Christian.

ALAN PATON

241

The Lord stands outside the door of every unyielded
room in your life, seeking entrance. If He enters, the door
must be opened from the inside.

RUTH PAXSON

242

We should never write off anything as impossible or as a failure. God gave us the capacity to think through any problem. The hopeful thinker projects hope and faith into the darkest situation and lights it up.

NORMAN VINCENT PEALE

243

You take on the image of the One you love.

BILL PEARCE

244

You are accepted by God, and here His love and tender care will be over you. His mercy will reach out to you daily and you shall have true satisfaction in your heart.

ISAAC PENNINGTON

245

God is always definite in His dealings with His children,
and the soul in fellowship with Him quickly knows when
He speaks with the still small voice of conscience; then it
must at once obey, and claim the cleansing of the precious
blood.

JESSE PENN-LEWIS

246

I don't see why anyone should settle for anything less than
Jacob, who actually grabbed aholt of God and wouldn't
let go until God identified Himself and blessed him.

WALKER PERCY

247

Evangelizing lost, secularized people is central to what is
on God's heart. It is a worthy obsession. Make it yours.

JIM PETERSEN

248

Obedience is rooted in love, not fear; it is activated by
affection, not by force. Keeping the commandments,
for Christians, is not dull rule-keeping but passionate
love-making. Each commandment is a channel
for expressing and sharing God's goodness.

EUGENE PETERSON

249

God is not the slightest degree baffled or bewildered by
what baffles and bewilders us. He is either a present help
or He is not much help at all.

J.B. PHILLIPS

250

The key to love and generosity is not primarily looking back on bygone grace and how much God has done for you—as precious and indispensable as that is. The key is to turn from the glory and guarantee of bygone grace and put your faith firmly in future grace.

JOHN PIPER

251

Nothing will be wasted if we give our lives to God. And if we are willing to be patient until the grace of God is made manifest. Whether it takes nine years or ninety, it will be worth the wait.

REBECCA MANLEY PIPPERT

252

God is true; His promises are sure to those who seek.

M.G. PLANTZ

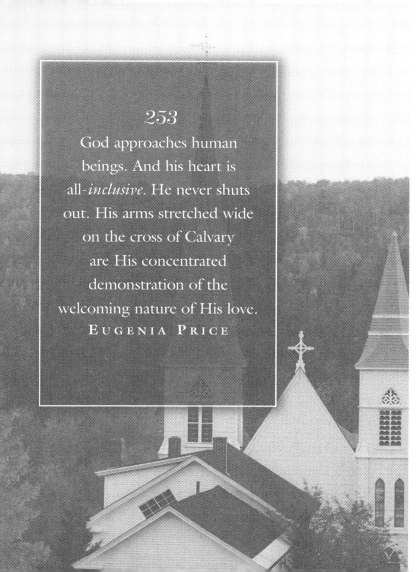

253

God approaches human beings. And his heart is all-*inclusive*. He never shuts out. His arms stretched wide on the cross of Calvary are His concentrated demonstration of the welcoming nature of His love.

EUGENIA PRICE

254

In all your actions think God sees thee, and in all His actions labor to see Him. That will make thee fear Him, and will move thee to love Him. The fear of God is the beginning of knowledge, and the knowledge of God is the perfection of love.

FRANCIS QUARLES

255

Each of us can continue to grow and enjoy the richness of life-giving love we receive from God and give to others. Our lifestyles will be forever changed as long as we allow Him to fill us up so we can give from that overflow.

LOIS RABEY

256

What a delightful sensation springs up in the mind when
the faculties and powers are engaged in promoting the
glory of Him who is invisible.

ROBERT RAIKES

257

We have no room here for the independent Christian;
we are engaged in one supreme task, that of reaching
this world for God, and it will take all of us.

ALAN REDPATH

258

How calmly we may commit ourselves to the hands of
Him who bears up the world.

JEAN PAUL RICHTER

259

When we have done all we can, we must still wait for God
to accomplish His purposes. As we wait, we can fix our
eyes on Jesus as a companion who empathizes with our
suffering and a Savior who is working behind the scenes.
Difficult circumstances seem to increase our ability to
experience intimacy with Christ.

RUTHANN RIDLEY

260

God does not allow us to continue to reduce Him to a size and shape we can manage. He moves in us in ways that burst our categories and overwhelm our finiteness. When we realize He's bigger than anything we can get our minds around, we can begin to relax and trust Him.

PAULA RINEHART

261

God speaks to us through our desires, then as we lay them at His feet, He helps us sort them out and quiets our hearts to accept what He has already prepared.

ROSALIND RINKER

262

To God we use the simplest, shortest words we can find
because eloquence is only air and noise to Him.

FREDERICK WILLIAM ROBERTSON

263

Your heart is the innermost part of you, the citadel of
your personality, the core and motivation of your being.
It is the deepest part of your spiritual life, the part that
makes everything else tick—and that part of you
must be centered totally on God.

PAT ROBERTSON

264

Christians alive to God, loving, caring, laughing,
sharing, involved at the point of people's need, present
an undeniable witness for Christ in their society.

HADDON W. ROBINSON

265

The devil may have the busy worker, or even the compelling preacher, but not, surely, the person whose heart is aglow with charity, ever eager to love God and indifferent to vanity.

RICHARD ROLLE

266

But God has never promised to keep us out of hard places. What He has promised is to go with us through every hard place, and to bring us through victoriously.

MERV ROSELL

267

Obedience is the fruit of faith;
patience, the bloom on the fruit.

CHRISTINA ROSSETTI

268

Why should I start at the plough of my Lord, that maketh the deep furrows on my soul? I know He is no idle husbandman, He purposeth a crop.

SAMUEL RUTHERFORD

269

The function of faith is to turn God's promises into facts.

J. OSWALD SANDERS

270

Scale the heights of a life abandoned to God, then you will look down on the clouds beneath your feet.

DARLOW SARGEANT

271

We can and must meditate on the Word of God, the Bible—His truth which gives us what we need to know for comfort and direction.

EDITH SCHAEFFER

272

We do not have a power plant inside ourselves that can
overcome the world. The overcoming is the work of the
Lord Jesus Christ. There can be a victory, a practical
victory, if we raise empty hands of faith,
moment by moment, and accept the gift.

FRANCIS SCHAEFFER

273

Dare to believe that God does love you. Believe it against
all odds. Dream against all dreams that God does care
about you and has a plan for your life
and wants you to succeed.

ROBERT A. SCHULLER

274

The Lord is never far away,
But, through all grief distressing,
An ever-present help and stay,
Our peace and joy and blessing.
As with a mother's tender hand
He leads His own,
His chosen band:
To God all praise and glory!

JOHANN JAKOB SCHÜTZ

275

No affliction or temptation, no
guilt nor power of sin, no wounded
spirit nor terrified conscience,
should induce us to despair of help
and comfort from God.

THOMAS SCOTT

276

Humility imparts a deep sense of our own weakness,
with a hearty and affectionate acknowledgment of our
owing all that we are to the divine bounty. It is
always accompanied by a profound submission
to the will of God, and great deadness toward
the glory of the world and applause of men.

HENRY SCOUGAL

277

God does not change the actual, factual nature of the
evil which occurs. But God can change the meaning
of it for your total life. God can weave it into the design
and purpose of your life, so that it all lies within the
circle of His redeeming and recycling activity.

DAVID A. SEAMANDS

278

God wants us to use Scripture in the way Jesus did. He wants us to store up His Word, which He infuses with power in present situations. He wants us to speak forth His Word, sending it into our problems.

JOHN SHERRILL

279

We must pray for eyes to see that even if the salvation of God is intensely personal, it is never private; to see that salvation includes God's concern for nations as well.

RON SIDER

280

Difficulties and obstacles are God's challenges to faith.
When hindrances confront us in the path of duty, we are
to recognize them as vessels for faith to fill with the
fullness and all-sufficiency of Jesus.

A.B. SIMPSON

281

The secret and reality of this blissful life in God cannot be
understood without receiving, living, and experiencing it.

SADHU SUNDAR SINGH

282

Christians, of all people, should reflect the mind of their
Maker. Learning to read well is a step toward loving
God with your mind. It is a leap toward thinking
God's thoughts after Him.

JAMES SIRE

283

God is unchangeable. He is as certain as the return of the high tide. To know that in our minds, even though our feelings are totally reserved, will be a help in restoring feelings of closeness to God. To focus on what is, rather than what we feel, is of vital importance.

ELIZABETH SKOGLUND

284

Forgiveness is God's invention for coming to terms with a world in which people are unfair to each other and hurt each other deeply. He began by forgiving us. And He invites us all to forgive each other.

LEWIS B. SMEDES

285

The more we experience of God's love, the more He
Himself becomes the primary desire and focus of our life.
The coercive aspects of the law become unnecessary. We
find ourselves longing to please God simply because
we love Him. And that is the greatest joy in life—
to experience a genuine love relationship with God.

CHUCK SMITH

286

Faith is not a thing to be seen, or touched, or handled.
It is not a grace, nor a gracious disposition. It is nothing
mysterious or perplexing. It is simply and only believing
God. And to "exercise faith" one has only to
exercise towards God the same believing
faculty one exercises towards man.

HANNAH WHITALL SMITH

287

He will not fail, nor mock, nor disappoint thee;
His consolations change not with the years;
With oil of joy He surely will anoint thee,
And wipe away thy tears.

J. DANSON SMITH

288

Are you in difficult circumstances, surrounded by people who do not understand you, who never consult your taste, who put you in the background? This thing is from Me. I am the God of circumstances. Thou camest not to thy place by accident, it is the very place God meant for thee.

LAURA A. SNOW

289

God does not call the qualified, He qualifies the called.

BETTY SOUTHARD

290

God's Word alone is the seed from which
all that is good in us must grow.

PHILIPP JAKOB SPENER

291

As sure as ever God puts His children in the furnace,
He will be in the furnace with them.

CHARLES HADDON SPURGEON

292

Both doing nothing, and doing too much, are a hindrance
to God's purpose. His will for the Christian is expressed in
the word *being,* which in turn will result in effective *doing.*

MILES STANFORD

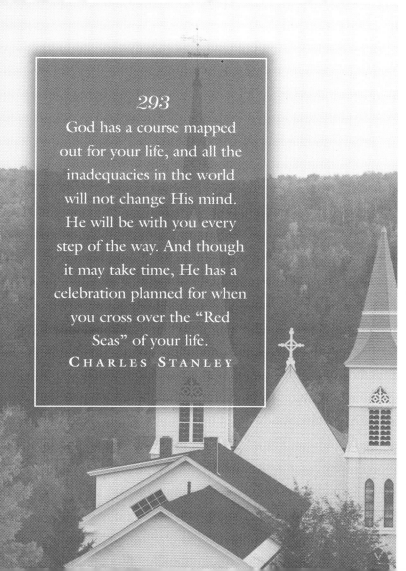

293

God has a course mapped
out for your life, and all the
inadequacies in the world
will not change His mind.
He will be with you every
step of the way. And though
it may take time, He has a
celebration planned for when
you cross over the "Red
Seas" of your life.

CHARLES STANLEY

294

In the school of adoration the soul learns why the
approach to every other goal had left it restless.

DOUGLAS V. STEERE

295

There is nothing but God's grace. We walk upon it;
we breathe it; we live and die by it.

ROBERT LOUIS STEVENSON

296

I find that it was easier to get Israel out of Egypt than to
get them into Canaan. Each step in advance evokes more
opposition than the previous step—but then God is
more and more to us as we advance, and this means
everything to the committed heart.

J.B. STONEY

297

God forgives not capriciously, but with wise, definite,
Divine prearrangement.

RICHARD SALTER STORRS

298

Our attempts at self-justification are as ineffectual as
[Adam and Eve's] fig leaves. We have to acknowledge
our nakedness, see the divine substitute wearing our
filthy rags instead of us, and allow Him to clothe us
with His own righteousness.

JOHN R.W. STOTT

299

Faith does nothing alone—nothing of itself,
but everything under God, by God, through God.

WILLIAM STOUGHTON

300

In all ranks of life the human heart yearns for the
beautiful; and the beautiful things that God makes
are His gift to all alike.

HARRIET BEECHER STOWE

301

If you have no joy in your religion,
there's a leak in your Christianity somewhere.

BILLY SUNDAY

302

God has given His children a wonderful freedom in
Christ, which means not only freedom from sin and
shame but also a freedom in lifestyle, so that
we can become models of His grace.

CHARLES R. SWINDOLL

303

Each of us is His special creation and is alive for a
distinctive purpose. Because of this, the person we are,
and the contribution we make by being that very person,
are vitally important to God.

LUCI SWINDOLL

304

Your suffering, like nothing else, has prepared you to
meet God—for what proof could you have brought
of your love if this life left you totally unscarred?

JONI EARECKSON TADA

305

Through all the changing scenes of life,
In trouble and in joy,
The praises of my God shall still
My heart and tongue employ.

NAHUM TATE

306
Pardon, not wrath, is God's best attribute.
BAYARD TAYLOR

307
I used to ask God to help me. Then I asked if
I might help Him. I ended up by asking Him
to do His work through me.
HUDSON TAYLOR

308
Humility begins as a gift from God,
but it is increased as a habit we develop.
JEREMY TAYLOR

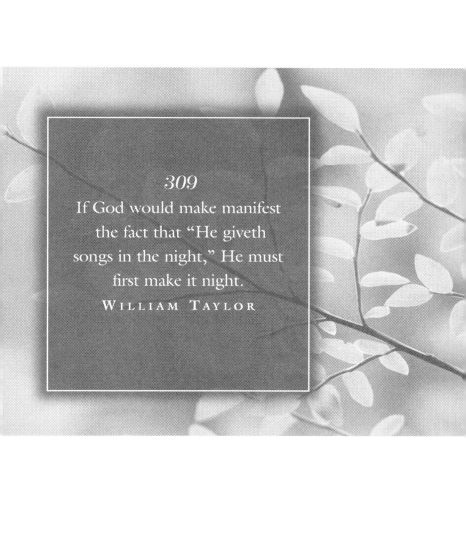

309
If God would make manifest
the fact that "He giveth
songs in the night," He must
first make it night.

WILLIAM TAYLOR

310

All Christian thinking must begin not with man,
but with God.

WILLIAM TEMPLE

311

Love is the result of an identification—the
identifying of our wills with the will of God,
and our destiny with that of all men,
however obscure, fallen and needy.

ROSE TERLIN

312

God will receive you, His own son, back, even if you
have squandered what you had received from Him,
even if you return naked—just because you *have*
returned; and will joy over your return.

TERTULLIAN

313

God wants to teach us how to please Him in every aspect of the chaos of reality. To this end He speaks to us clearly when we take time to listen believingly. He wants to bring all of who He is to bear on all of who we are.

MARTHA THATCHER

314

We are called Christians because we are anointed with the unction of God.

THEOPHILUS

315

There is no more sensitive conscience than that of
a person who loves God. It registers every shadow
that passes over the heart of God.

HELMUT THIELICKE

316

In the practice of prayer one is escorted further
and deeper into knowing and loving God.

BECKY TIRABASSI

317

God does not want His children to be in a state of condemnation before Him. He wishes us to be free from all care, worry, anxiety, and self-condemnation. Any earthly parent would make the way clear to his child who asked to know it, and much more will our heavenly Father make it clear to us.

R. A. TORREY

318

God's way of thinking is different from ours. And the
whole point is that we should take the great leap
from our own thoughts to those of God.

PAUL TOURNIER

319

Even if we wanted to, we could not manipulate God.
We fast and pray for results,
but the results are in God's hands.

ELMER L. TOWNS

320

It is most important to our spiritual warfare that we hold in our minds a right conception of God. If we think of Him as cold and exacting, we shall find it impossible to love Him. If again, we hold Him to be kind and understanding, our whole inner life will mirror that idea.

A.W. TOZER

321

When we know God's love, we will become the
persons He wants us to be. He does not patch
up our virtues, but creates a new person.

INGRID TROBISCH

322

We need to walk on the earth as Jesus walked, and meet
people where they are. After we have been born on this
earth, we have to be born again, but God isn't finished
with us. He wants us to be born a third time, back
from the spiritual to just being human again.

WALTER TROBISCH

323

This is the way God meets every real
sacrifice of every child of His.
We surrender all and accept poverty;
and He sends wealth. We renounce a
rich field of service; He sends us a
richer one than we had dared to
dream of. We give up our cherished
hopes and die unto self; He sends
us the life more abundant,
and tingling joy.

C.G. TRUMBALL

324

When circumstances seem impossible, when all signs of grace in you seem at their lowest ebb, when temptation is fiercest, when love and joy and hope seem well-nigh extinguished in your heart, then rest, without feeling and without emotion, in the Father's faithfulness.

D. TRYON

325

As Christians, we cannot sit about wringing our hands in helplessness. We are not impotent. We can work mightily for justice, peace, and reconciliation. After all, we are the instruments of God's peace.

DESMOND TUTU

326

Faith is, then, a lively and steadfast trust in the favour of
God, wherewith we commit ourselves together unto God.
And that trust is so surely grounded and sticks so fast in
our hearts, that a man would not once doubt of it,
although he should die a thousand times therefor.

WILLIAM TYNDALE

327

The determined fixing of our will upon God, and pressing
toward Him steadily and without deflection; this is
the very center and the art of prayer.

EVELYN UNDERHILL

328

God is no fault-finder, always looking for things to con-
demn in us. He estimates us at our best, not our worst.

THE UPPER ROOM

329

The cross that Jesus tells us to carry is the one that we
willingly take up ourselves—the cross of self-denial in
order that we might live for the glory of the Father.

COLIN URQUHART

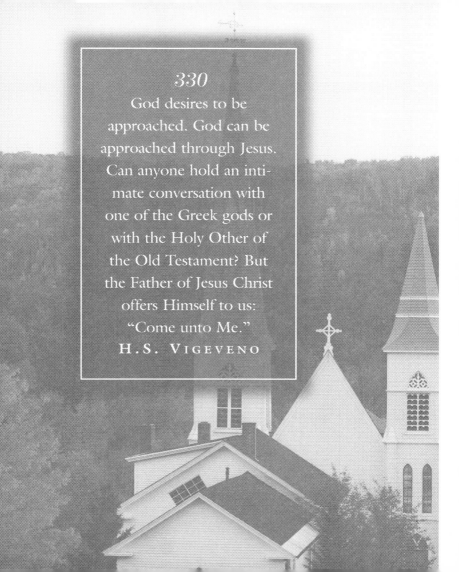

330

God desires to be approached. God can be approached through Jesus. Can anyone hold an intimate conversation with one of the Greek gods or with the Holy Other of the Old Testament? But the Father of Jesus Christ offers Himself to us: "Come unto Me."

H.S. VIGEVENO

331

He commonly brings His help in our greatest extremity,
that His finger may plainly appear in our deliverance.
And this method He chooses that we may not trust upon
anything that we see or feel, as we are always apt to do,
but only His bare Word, which we may depend
upon in every state.

C.H. VON BOGATZKY

332

If you feel stuck, bring your whole self to Christ, not just
the problem, but you. Ask God to change your heart.
Commit yourself to pray to that end. It's God's heart
to give good gifts to His children.

SHEILA WALSH

333

We talk with God, not just to Him. God talks with us too,
causing a circle to be whole and closed between us.

WALTER WANGERIN JR.

334

God's never been guilty of sponsoring a flop.

ETHEL WATERS

335

The closer we get to God,
the more we prize the individual soul.

G.D. WATSON

336

Were the whole realm of nature mine,
That were a present far too small;
Love so amazing, so divine,
Demands my soul, my life, my all.

ISAAC WATTS

337

Don't trust to hold God's hand; let Him hold yours. Let
Him do the holding, and you the trusting.

HAMMER WILLIAM WEBB-PEPLOE

338

There are three things that only God knows: the beginning of things, the cause of things, and the end of things.

WELSH PROVERB

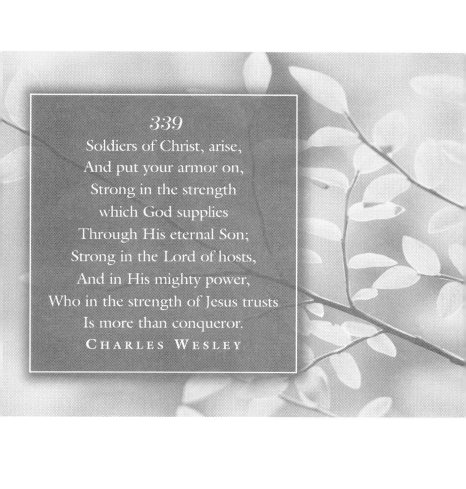

339

Soldiers of Christ, arise,
And put your armor on,
Strong in the strength
which God supplies
Through His eternal Son;
Strong in the Lord of hosts,
And in His mighty power,
Who in the strength of Jesus trusts
Is more than conqueror.

CHARLES WESLEY

340
Whatever good is in man, or is done by man, God is the
author and doer of it.
JOHN WESLEY

341
God is such an infinite blessing that every sense of His
glorious presence gives gladness to the heart. Every step
toward Him is, likewise, a measure of happiness.
SUSANNA WESLEY

342
Lord, through this house, be Thou our Guide,
so by Thy power, no foot shall slide.
WESTMINSTER CHIMES

343

Determine to be an encouragement to everyone whom God brings across your path. It costs little to say a kind word and to communicate a sense of support. But like the girl who doesn't want to encourage a suitor, we fear that kind words will lead to further demands. Such is the risk.

JERRY WHITE

344

Faith and hope in God bring prayer alive and make it persistent. Both virtues, faith and hope, come to us when Scripture is stored in our minds and hearts.

JOHN WHITE

345

They who joy in God have a joy that strangers inter-
meddle not with—it is a joy that no man can take
from them; it amounts to a full assurance of faith
that the soul is reconciled to God.

GEORGE WHITEFIELD

346

Prayer is a rising up and drawing near to God in mind,
and in heart, and in spirit.

ALEXANDER WHYTE

347

Desire toward God, and you will have desires from God.
He will meet you on the line of those desires when you
reach out in simple faith.

SMITH WIGGLESWORTH

348

No sin the believer brings
to God, when it comes to
being weighed, is not
greatly outweighed by
the blood of Christ.

G.V. WIGRAM

349

God·insists that He set up
His throne in the heart,
and reign in it, without a
rival. If we keep Him from
His right, it will matter not
by what competitor.

WILLIAM WILBERFORCE

350

God's Word does more than draw us near to Him. It is our life. Mankind does not live by bread alone, but by every word that proceeds from the mouth of God.

ANN WILCOX

351

Christ's love is a love without angles; a love that asks nothing in return … this is the quality that redeems.

DAVID WILKERSON

352

With this magnificent God positioned among us, Jesus brings us the assurance that our universe is a perfectly safe place to be.

DALLAS WILLARD

353

The strong hands of God twisted the crown of thorns into
a crown of glory; and in such hands we are safe.

CHARLES WILLIAMS

354

God gives His servants a taste in this life, yet the harvest
and the vintage are to come, when they that suffer
with Christ Jesus shall reign with Him, and they
that have sown in tears shall reap the
never-ending harvest of inconceivable joys.

ROGER WILLIAMS

355

O Lord, forgive what I have been,
sanctify what I am, and order what I shall be.

THOMAS WILSON

356

In this broken world we will often experience two emotions at once: sadness at sin, but at the same time rejoicing at what God is doing in us and in the world and what He is going to do in the future.

RICHARD WINTER

357

Lord, be thy word my rule,
In it may I rejoice,
Thy glory be my aim,
Thy holy will be my choice.

CHRISTOPHER WORDSWORTH

358

Pray to God at the beginning of all thy works that thou mayest bring them all to a good ending.

XENOPHON

359

God is able. I have no one save the
Holy Ghost to rely upon.
KIYE SATO YAMAMURO

360

The same God who created the
heavens and earth has the power to
bridge the great chasm that separates
Him from His creatures. He will
reconcile, He will forgive, no matter
what obstacles His prodigal
children put in the way.
PHILIP YANCEY

361

God may be in the process of pruning something out of your life at this very moment. If this is the case, don't fight it. Instead, welcome it, for His pruning will make you more fruitful and bring greater glory to the Father.

RICK YOHN

362

Who worships God shall find him. Humble love,
And not proud reason, keeps the door of heaven;
Love finds admission, where proud science fails.

EDWARD YOUNG

363

If we do not listen we do not come to truth.
If we do not pray we do not even get as far as listening.

HUBERT VAN ZELLER

364

He leads us on through all the unquiet years;
Past all our dreamland hopes, and doubts and fears,
He guides our steps, through all the tangled maze
Of losses, sorrows, and o'erclouded days;
We know His will is done;
And still He leads us on.

N.L. ZINZENDORF

365

The fear of the Lord, which is the beginning of wisdom,
consists in a complete devotion to God.

OTTO ZOCKLER

About the Compiler

Judith Couchman owns Judith & Company, a writing and editing business. She has also served as the creator and founding editor-in-chief of *Clarity* magazine, managing editor of *Christian Life,* editor of *Sunday Digest,* director of communications for The Navigators, and director of new product development for NavPress.

Besides speaking to women's and professional groups, Judith is the author or compiler of thirty-five books and many magazine articles. In addition, she has received numerous awards for her work in secondary education, religious publishing, and corporate communications.

She lives in Colorado.